Mini Mike
in the Old Testament

by Carl Anker Mortensen

Illustrated by José Pérez Montero

SCANDINAVIA PUBLISHING HOUSE

Mini Mike
in the Old Testament

Copyright © 1995
  Scandinavia Publishing House
  Drejervej 15, 3
  DK- 2400 Copenhagen NV
  Denmark

E-mail: jvo@scanpublishing.dk
Phone +45 35 31 03 30

Text: Carl Anker Mortensen

English: Marlee Alex
  and Anne de Graaf

Illustrations: José Pérez Montero

Graphic design: Nils V. Glistrup

Printed in Singapore

ISBN 87 7247 439 4

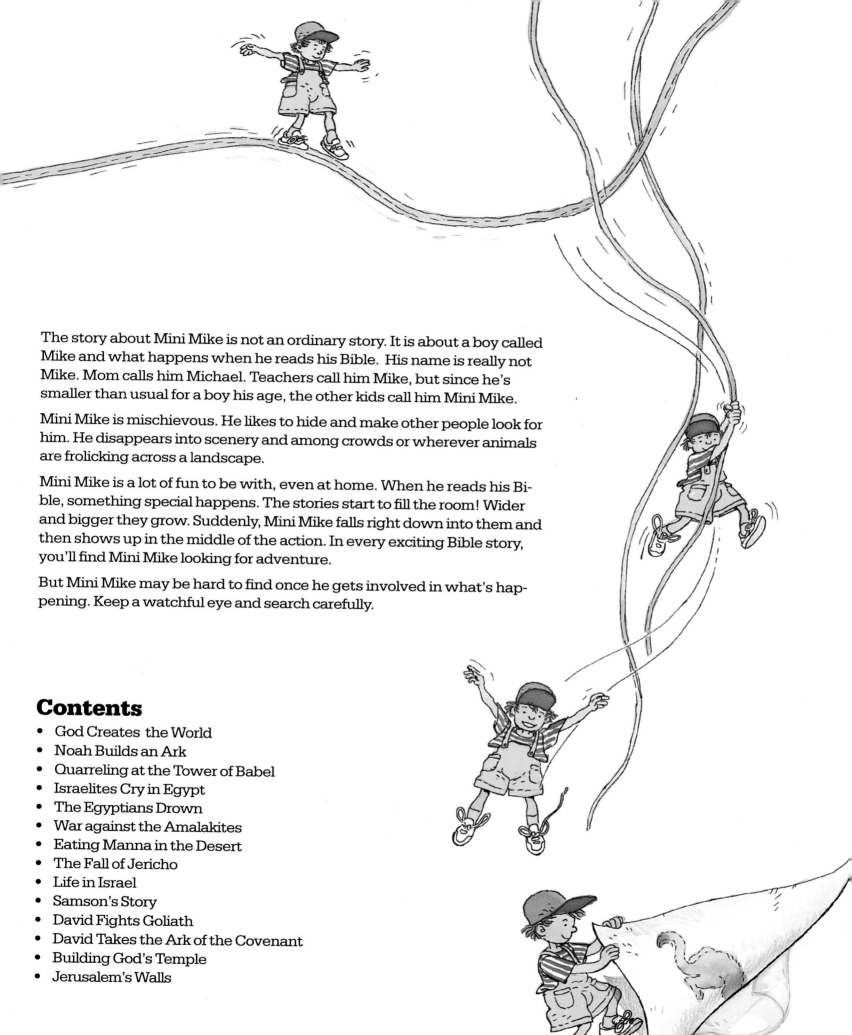

The story about Mini Mike is not an ordinary story. It is about a boy called Mike and what happens when he reads his Bible. His name is really not Mike. Mom calls him Michael. Teachers call him Mike, but since he's smaller than usual for a boy his age, the other kids call him Mini Mike.

Mini Mike is mischievous. He likes to hide and make other people look for him. He disappears into scenery and among crowds or wherever animals are frolicking across a landscape.

Mini Mike is a lot of fun to be with, even at home. When he reads his Bible, something special happens. The stories start to fill the room! Wider and bigger they grow. Suddenly, Mini Mike falls right down into them and then shows up in the middle of the action. In every exciting Bible story, you'll find Mini Mike looking for adventure.

But Mini Mike may be hard to find once he gets involved in what's happening. Keep a watchful eye and search carefully.

Contents

God Creates the World

God is busy creating the animals when Mike shows up. Now we're in for some fun. Mike has never even seen most of these animals. Do you recognize the one he's sitting on? What is it called? Remember, at this point in time, Mike is the only person in the whole wide world; even Adam and Eve had not yet been created when Mike arrived here.

Questions

1. Can you find the animals wearing pants?
2. Find the lions being a family.
3. Which animals are wearing hats?
4. What is the largest elephant doing?
5. How many of the animals do you recognize?
   What are they called?
   What would you call them, if you were naming the animals?

Read

Genesis 1: 24-25

God made the wild animals according to their kinds, the livestock according to their kinds, and all the creatures that move along the ground according to their kinds. And God saw that it was good. — GENESIS 1:25

4

Noah Builds an Ark

Here is Noah. God has given him the job of building a large boat. It's called an ark. When the rain starts falling, every living being who doesn't make it into the ark will drown. It is God's punishment for those who choose not to listen to Him and follow His ways. Can you see Noah? He is trying to get two of every kind of animal into the ark. Noah's family is going to be safe on board. But where is Mike? Will he also be rescued from the flood?

Questions

1. Find Noah. What do you think he is doing?
2. How many different animals are on their way into the ark?
3. How are the parrots getting in?
4. What makes you think that Noah is expecting the rains to start soon?
5. Find Mrs. Noah. What is she afraid of?

Read

Genesis 6:13-22

I am going to bring floodwaters on the earth to destroy all life under the heavens, every creature that has breath of life in it ... But I will establish my covenant with you, and you will enter the ark. — GENESIS 6:17-18

Quarreling at the Tower of Babel

There are lots of people here, all gathered together in one place. Is Mike here, too? The people are trying to build a tower so high that it reaches clear up to heaven. Do you think they'll manage to finish it? This does not please God. He stops them by suddenly making them speak many different languages at one time. No one can understand what the person next to him is saying. The people can't work together on building the tower. Mike is looking for someone who speaks English. Can you find him?

Questions

1. Can you find the missing horseshoe?
2. What game do you think the children are playing with the camel?
3. Find the man with the bad foot. What happened?
4. What are they building the tower out of?
5. Guess how many persons there are in the picture. Count them one by one.
6. Can you say "Get to work!" in a foreign language?

Read

Genesis 11:1-9

Come, let us build ourselves a city, with a tower that reaches to the heavens, so that we may make a name for ourselves and not be scattered over the face of the whole earth. – GENESIS 11:4

8

Israelites Cry in Egypt

These people are the people of God. They come from the land of Israel. One time when they had nothing to eat in their country, they traveled all the way to Egypt to find food. After many years in Egypt, many, many children, grandchildren and great-grandchildren were born to them. Pharaoh, the king of Egypt, made slaves out of the people of Israel. Can you see the whips he used on them? Mike is hiding from the slave-masters. You probably would, too, if you were there.

Questions

1. What are the animals doing?
2. Find all the Egyptians with whips. How many are there?
3. Look for other Egyptians. What are they doing?
4. What kind of work do the women do?
5. Do the children work hard too?
6. Who is not working? Really?

Read

Exodus 1:7-14

The Israelites groaned in their slavery and cried out, and their cry for help because of their slavery went up to God.

— *Exodus 2:23*

The Egyptians Drown

When Moses led the people of Israel out of Egypt, king Pharaoh sent the Egyptian army to bring them back. God rescued all the men, women and children by helping them cross the Red Sea through a narrow pathway of dry land. When the Egyptian army followed though, the sea walls collapsed and all the soldiers drowned, while God's people were safe on the other side. Mike is cheering for the Israelites. Can you see him?

Questions

1. Can you find the artist painting a picture? What is he painting?
2. Look for the vender. What do you think he is selling?
3. How many drowning horses can you count?
4. Find the happy Israelites. Why do you think they are so happy?
5. Look for the boy on the scooter.
6. Which way do the Israelites go now?

Read

Exodus 14:21-30

The water flowed back and covered the chariots and horsemen – the entire army of Pharaoh that had followed the Israelites into the sea. Not one of them survived. — EXODUS 14:29

War against the Amalakites

There is a war going on here. The enemy is a tribe called the Amalakites. God's people, the people of Israel, are fighting hard. Mike wants to see who will win. He is watching the man named Moses who is holding his hands in the air. As long as Moses holds his arms up, the Israelites will keep on winning. Maybe you can guess who is helping them win.

Questions

1. Can you find the man taking a shower?
2. Find the warrior pleading for mercy for his life.
3. Find the sick-wagons.
4. Look for the fire. Do you think the tent will burn down?
5. Look for the vender. What is he selling? Is he the same man as the vender by the Red Sea?

Read

Exodus 17:8-13

As long as Moses held up his hands, the Israelites were winning, but whenever he lowered his hands, the Amalakites were winning. — EXODUS 17:11

14

Eating Manna in the Desert

The Israelites are on a long journey – going home to their own country. They have been camping in tents and wandering in the desert for a long time. They've just discovered that God has provided a new kind of food for them. It is lying on the ground and looks like snow. But it's really a kind of bread called manna. Mike is finding out that it tastes good.

Questions

1. How can you tell that it is not winter?
2. Find the man with the snow-pusher. What is he doing?
3. Look for the man with skis and ski poles.
4. Find out if the animals also eat the manna.
5. How many happy people can you find?
6. When was the last time you tasted a new food?

Read

Exodus 16:12-16

Thin flakes like frost on the ground appeared on the desert floor ... Moses said to them, "It is the bread the Lord has given you to eat." — EXODUS 16:14-15

The Fall of Jericho

The Israelites are back in Israel where they belong. This town is called Jericho. Can you see what is happening? God told His people to walk around the town for six days. Today is the seventh day. After the seventh time around, they shouted with all their might and blew loudly on their horns. When they did that, God made the big wall around the town crumble and fall down. Mike looks frightened. Is he running away?

Questions

1. How many different trumpets can you find? Can you find more than eight?
2. What else is making noise?
3. Who is walking at the front of the army?
4. Can you find any children in the crowd?
5. How many times have they walked around the walls so far?
6. Why did Jericho have a wall around it?

Read

Joshua 6:1-20

When the trumpets sounded, the people shouted, and at the sound of the trumpet, when the people gave a loud shout, the wall collapsed. — JOSHUA 6:20

Life in Israel

Back in Israel, the people of God are living happily in freedom. This is different than living as slaves in Egypt. They love to work here, making their fields grow and bear fruit. They are working on the grape harvest now. They use huge boxes. Mike is enjoying himself. Do you like grapes, too?

Questions

1. Find the men in the huge basin. What are they doing?
2. Find some children. Are they working on the grape harvest too?
3. What kind of working animals do you find?
4. Find the man enjoying life.
5. What do you think they use the pitchers for?

Read

Joshua 24:13

When the Lord your God brings you into the land he swore to your fathers ... then when you eat and are satisfied be careful that you do not forget the Lord, who brought you out of Egypt.
— DEUTERONOMY 6:10-12

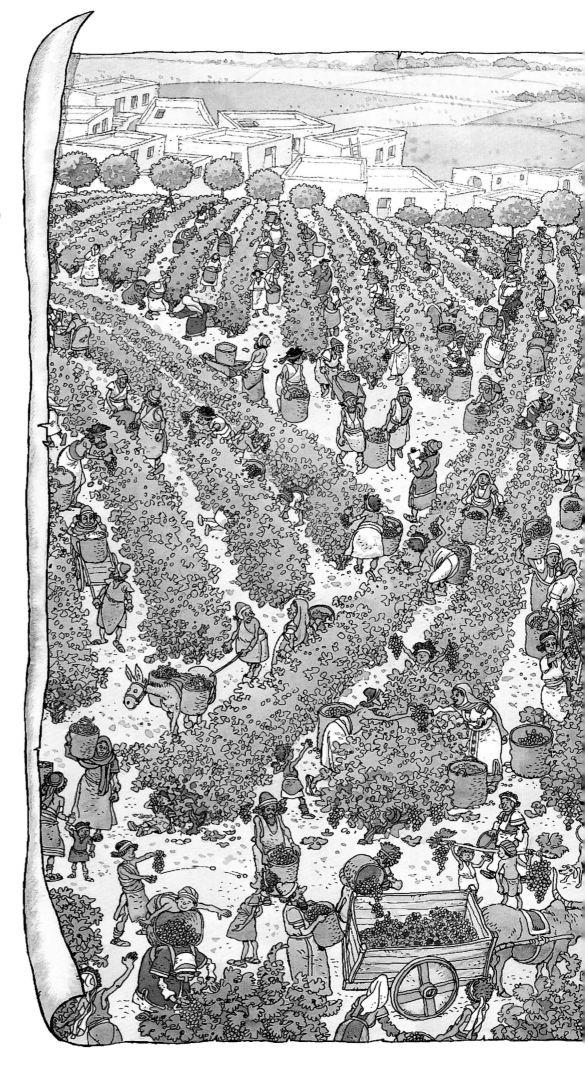

Samson's Story

These people are Philistines, the worst enemies of the Israelites. But the man standing between the columns is not a Philistine. His name is Samson. The Philistines have put his eyes out. When Samson's hair is long, as it is now, God makes him strong. Whoops, can you see Mike is sneaking away? In a moment, Samson will push the columns down so the entire building crashes down. This is Samson's way of defeating the Philistines.

Questions

1. Look for the balloon man. How many balloons do you see?
2. Find the two cameramen.
3. Locate the people hiding under a table.
4. Find the lady wearing glasses.
5. Find the man who is kneeling.
6. Have you found anyone smiling?

Read

Judges 16:23-30

Samson said to the servant who held his hand, 'Put me where I can feel the pillars that support the temple, so that I may lean against them.' Now the temple was crowded with men and women: all the rulers of the Philistines were there, and on the roof were about three thousand men and women watching Samson perform. Then Samson prayed to the Lord, 'O Sovereign Lord, remember me. O God, please strengthen me just once more ...' Then Samson reached towards the two central pillars on which the temple stood ... Then he pushed with all his might, and down came the temple on the rulers and all the people in it. Thus he killed many more when he died than while he lived.

— JUDGES 16:26-30

David Fights Goliath

Here lies Goliath, a giant soldier from the Philistine army! He no longer swears at God or makes jokes about David, the shepherd boy. David has killed him with a slingshot and one stone. The stone hit Goliath right in the forehead. Now the Israelites are jumping for joy and so is Mike.

Questions

1. Can you see the pile of weapons? Why do you think the Israelites left them there?
2. Why do you think one of the men is leaving the picture?
3. David is holding Goliath's sword. What do you think he will do with it?
4. How can you find out who the Israelites are?
5. Find the Philistine man biting his fingernails. What is he afraid of?

Read

1 Samuel 17:32-54

Reaching into his bag and taking out a stone, he slung it and struck the Philistine on the forehead. The stone sank into his forehead, and he fell face down on the ground. So David triumphed over the Philistine with a sling and a stone.
— *1 SAMUEL 17:49-50*

David Takes the Ark of the Covenant

Mike has arrived at a party! It is a party to celebrate bringing the ark of the covenant back to Jerusalem, the capital of Israel. David is king now, he is the first one in line, dancing with joy. The pure gold ark is the most important holy thing for the Jews. It is kept in the most holy place, the temple. The Jews believed, where the ark is, God lives. Now God will be in the middle of the holy city of Jerusalem. Everyone is happy. Can you see Mike dancing, too?

Questions

1. How many different musical instruments can you find? There are eight.
2. Look for a funny bicycle.
3. Find the tourist guide.
4. What are they using for a frisbee?
5. Find the kids playing wheelbarrow.
6. Give a reason why you should dance for joy.

Read

2 Samuel 6:1-19

David danced before the Lord with all his might while he and the entire house of Israel brought up the ark of the Lord with shouts and the sound of trumpets. — 2 SAMUEL 6:14-15

Building God's Temple

These people are building a temple. Before King David died, he had arranged for all the materials needed. His son, Solomon, is king now. God told Solomon exactly how to build the temple. It is going to be big. It's good there are many construction workers and craftsmen to do the work. Mike won't be much help. But he's going to hang around and watch.

Questions

1. Can you find workers on roller skates?
2. How many different animals are being used in the work?
3. Look for the line of workers carrying stones. How many are there?
4. How did they find out what the temple should look like?
5. Why is smoke coming out of the chimney?
6. What else was Solomon famous for?

Read

1 King 6

... the temple was finished in all its details according to its specifications. He had spent seven years building it. – 1 KING 6:38

Jerusalem's Walls

Have you ever seen so many builders working on a project? The walls of Jerusalem have been destroyed by Israel's enemies and the gates were burned to the ground. Mike is speaking with someone. The man's name is Nehemiah. Nehemiah is directing the whole operation, rebuilding the giant walls of Jerusalem. It is important for Israel to rebuild the walls so they will be safe from their enemies.

Questions

1. Can you find the man carrying his donkey on his shoulders?
2. Where is the man on a skateboard?
3. Find a mouse.
4. Can you find the boy pulling a cat by the tail?
5. Find a kangaroo in the picture.
6. Look for the man taking a video.
7. How many different animals are you able to find? How about seven?
8. Can you point out the man with a sword in his belt?

Read

Nehemiah 3:

So the wall was completed – When all our enemies heard about this and all the surrounding nations saw it, our enemies lost their self-confidence, because they realized that this work had been done with the help of our God. — NEHEMIAH 6:15-16

Here are some of the things Mini Mike found on his journey through the Old Testament. Unfortunately, he can't remember where he found them. Can you help him out?

Questions

 Is this a flower? If not, what is it?

 What kind of animal is this?

 This will be extremely hard to find. Do you think you can do it?

 Why are they together?

 What is this for?

 This looks like a lamp. Do you think that's what it is?

 There are several dogs in this book. Where do you find this one?

 This animal is easy to recognize, but can you find it?

 Don't you think this man is hardworking?

 What do you think was in this bag?

 Guess who this belongs to. What is it?

 This pair of shoes belongs on whose feet?

 Can you imagine what this contains?

 Where do you find this tray?